Explaining God's Will For Your Life

Bruce D. Reekie

Sovereign World

Copyright © Bruce D. Reekie 1991

All rights reserved. No part of this publication may be reproduced, stored in a retrieval system, or transmitted, in any form or by any means, electronic, mechanical, photocopying, recording or otherwise, without the prior permission of the publisher.

Short extracts may be used for review purposes.

Scripture quotations are from the following versions, as indicated in the text:
NKJV   New King James Version of the Bible.
Copyright © 1983 Thomas Nelson, Inc.
KJV   King James Version.
NIV   New International Version.
Copyright © 1973, 1978, International Bible Society, published by Hodder and Stoughton.
TCNT   The Twentieth Century New Testament.
KNOX   The Holy Bible: A translation from the Latin Vulgate in the Light of the Hebrew and Greek Originals (Monsignor Ronald Knox).

ISBN: 1-85240-072-2

Production & Printing in England for
SOVEREIGN WORLD LIMITED
P.O. Box 17, Chichester, West Sussex PO20 6YB
by Nuprint Ltd, Station Road, Harpenden, Herts AL5 4SE.

To Heather,
my loving wife
and
chief encourager.

Contents

	Foreword	7
1	The Premise Of Life	9
2	The Power Of Life	14
3	The Parameter Of Life	18
4	The Seedbed Of Fruitfulness	22
5	An Attitude	27
6	A Time And A Place	30
7	A Sphere	34
8	A Dedicated Life	39
9	A Renewed Mind	42
10	The Value Of Godly Counsel	50
11	How To Discern The Will Of God	54
12	The Witness Of The Spirit	58
13	The Providence Of God	63
14	Birthing The Will Of God Through Intercessory Prayer	67

Foreword

The youthful C.H. Spurgeon once made a suggestion to a conference of ministers only to be told by an older colleague that he should go home until his beard had grown. The quick witted C.H.S., with the incredible knowledge of scripture and ability at repartee, for which he later became famous, simply pointed out that the Old Testament incident (1 Chronicles 19:5) to which the older minister alluded had nothing to do with youth but referred to the older men who had lost something in battle.

The author, Bruce Reekie, though comparatively a young man is full bearded, both naturally, when I last saw him, and spiritually. And the thing I like about his first book is that it is scripturally based. None of this experimental stuff which has little or no foundation in scripture. In dealing with his topic of Ministry within the Will of God, Bruce takes a simple and concise look at the teaching of the Bible. Being simple the truths are readily grasped. Being concise it doesn't take ages to read. In fact it occurred to me that you could take one chapter per day for two weeks as your daily devotional.

As a fifth generation Pentecostal who has been reared on the Word in the atmosphere of the Spirit, the author certainly has something to contribute. I enjoyed reading the fourteen chapters of the manuscript and commend the book to you. Obviously it's not the last word on what is surely the most important facet of Christian ministry. But it is a part of the learning process in which we are all disciples. I look forward to more insights from Bruce's pen.

Philip L. Powell
National General Secretary, Assemblies of God in Australia.
Editor of the Australian Evangel.

1

The Premise Of Life

You are worthy, O Lord, To receive glory and honour and power; For You created all things, And by Your will they exist and were created. (Revelation 4:11)

With characteristic authority and simplicity, the Bible declares that all things were created by God's will. In fact, the will of God is the sole reason for the existence of man. The will of God is indeed, the premise of life. Apart from God's will, nothing can live, move or have its being, in heaven or on earth.

The principle of dependency on the will of God governs both the natural and the spiritual creation. The Apostle John declared:

But as many as received Him, to them He gave the right to become children of God, to those who believe in His name: who were born, not of blood, nor of the will of the flesh, nor of the will of man, but of God.

(John 1:12,13)

In evangelical circles we speak about 'making a decision for Christ,' or 'choosing to follow Jesus.' However, in so doing, we put the cart before the horse. Jesus said, *'No one can come to Me unless the Father who sent Me draws Him'* (John 6:44).

It is only through the will of God that a man or a woman

can be born again. *'Of His own will He brought us forth by the Word of truth'* (James 1:18). Spiritual life, like natural life, is based upon and derived from the will of God.

There is only one source of life in the universe—the Lord God. Oh, how much we owe to His goodwill! It is because of the will of God that we have life, both physical and eternal. And it is because of the will of God that you are alive today!

You are not an accident, a meaningless cog in the cosmic machine. You are here by Divine appointment. You have a destiny in Christ Jesus. You have a future in the will of God!

The life of Paul

One of the most outstanding men in the Bible was undoubtedly the Apostle Paul. I am constantly challenged by Paul's philosophy of life and ministry, so evident in his letters to the churches. He often commenced an epistle by acknowledging the source of his life and the foundation of his ministry.

> *Paul called to be an apostle of Jesus Christ through the will of God.* (1 Corinthians 1:1)

Paul recognised that in his life and ministry, everything depended on, was sustained by and was regulated according to the will of God. Paul was very conscious of God's sovereign hand upon his life.

In Galatians chapter one, Paul says, *'God separated me from my mother's womb... called me through His grace... and revealed His Son in me when it pleased Him.'* Hardly the testimony of modern-day Christians!

Paul recognised that he could not do or be anything apart from God's plan for his life. To persist in his own way would inevitably lead to destruction.

Only one will

In the life of the Christian there is only one will that counts—God's will. The notion that 'it doesn't matter what you do as long as you are involved in the Lord's work and do it for His glory' is wrong, absolutely wrong. And it is the cause of much heartache and frustration and many a shipwreck in the lives of God's people.

We are not called to be busy—rather, we are called to 'wait on the Lord', and in waiting on the Lord, to hear His voice and discover His will for our lives.

Please don't misunderstand me. I am not saying that we don't have to work in the Kingdom of God. However, our work begins when the will of God is revealed. Until that time, we should wait in His Presence for His instruction and direction.

Much time, effort and money is wasted because we don't have ears to hear what the Spirit is saying to the churches. Sin is 'missing the mark' or 'falling short' of God's standard of holiness and His will for our lives.

People 'miss the mark' not only in terms of violating God's moral laws, but also in terms of performing 'dead works'—doing things God has not called them to do. Too often we undertake projects, erect buildings and pursue goals in the name of the Lord, but without His authority or approval. It might sound noble and appear valiant, but if God hasn't told you to do it, leave it alone!

Jesus recognised the subtlety of this problem and dealt with it in His teaching on the Kingdom of God, otherwise known as 'The sermon on the mount':

> *Not everyone who says to me, 'Lord, Lord', shall enter the Kingdom of Heaven, but he who does the will of My Father in heaven. Many will say to Me in that day, 'Lord, Lord, have we not prophesied in Your name, cast out demons in Your name, and done many wonders in*

> *Your name?' And then I will declare to them, 'I never knew you; depart from Me, you who practice lawlessness!'* (Matthew 7:21–23)

Notice that Jesus did not dispute their claims. However, the implication of His reply is clear: 'I never knew you... I never authorised you... I never approved of you... I didn't tell you to do it.'

Jesus calls those who act on their own initiative, apart from His authority and outside the parameters of God's will, 'practitioners of lawlessness'. The Kingdom of Heaven, on the other hand, is made up of the humble and obedient—those who are submitted to the Father's will.

The will of God is the only premise on which to build a fruitful and enduring life and ministry. If one builds on the clear and specific instruction of the Lord, one is building on a sure foundation that will survive any kind of Satanic or human storm.

But if one builds on a revelation that God gave to someone else, or on a calling that someone else received, or on a method that someone else employed, one will fall in the day of adversity.

Jesus warned that *'every plant which My Heavenly Father has not planted will be uprooted'* (Matthew 15:13). You had better be sure that your life and ministry—all that you are saying and doing in Jesus' name—is based on the foundation of God's revealed will for your life. Otherwise, it will not last.

The example of Christ

Our Lord Jesus Christ is of course, the ultimate example of a life fully committed to the will of God. Jesus expressed the whole focus, desire and dedication of His life in the Gospel of John, chapter five and verse thirty:

> *I can of Myself do nothing. As I hear, I judge; and My judgment is righteous, because I do not seek My own will but the will of the Father who sent Me.* (John 5:30)

As a result of His commitment to the will of God, Jesus glorified the Father on earth and finished the work the Father gave Him to do.

The will of God is the basis for fruitfulness and longevity, in both life and ministry. May we be numbered among those who do the will of God and abide forever!

2

The Power Of Life

In the Gospel of John, chapter four, we read about Jesus' encounter with the woman of Samaria. Jesus had left Judea and was returning to Galilee, via Samaria, a distance of approximately 20 miles. It was a long and toilsome journey across a somewhat difficult country. The Bible indicates that Jesus arrived at Jacob's well tired, hungry and thirsty.

However, an event occurred at Jacob's well that not only caused Jesus to forget His immediate needs, but supernaturally replenished His strength and energy.

The disciples left Jesus sitting by the well and went on into the city to buy food. Meanwhile, along came a woman of Samaria to draw water. Jesus said to her, 'Give me a drink.'

It is clear that Jesus' ultimate purpose in asking for a drink was not to satisfy His thirst, but to engage this woman in conversation with a view to ministering to her deep spiritual need.

As the conversation progressed, Jesus began to probe the depths of her soul with revelation knowledge given to Him by the Holy Spirit. He addressed her deep hunger for spiritual reality and spoke of the living water of everlasting life which only He could give.

He dealt compassionately but firmly with the immoral life she was leading, and directed her attention beyond religious externals to the one thing that really mattered—a relationship with God the Father.

Throughout the course of the conversation the

Samaritan's attitude was gradually changing—from one of cultural hostility and defensive pride to curiosity, and then conviction, and finally faith in Jesus as the Christ, the Saviour of the world.

At this point the disciples returned and found Jesus concluding His conversation with the Samaritan. Realising how hungry He must have been, they urged Him to eat some of the food they had obtained in the city.

But Jesus showed no interest in the food they had brought; in fact, He wasn't hungry anymore. He said to them, *'I have food to eat of which you do not know.'* The disciples were quite bewildered and said to one another, *'Has anyone brought Him anything to eat?'*

Jesus responded by teaching them a fundamental principle of living and ministering in the will of God:

> *My food is to do the will of Him who sent Me, and to finish His work. Do you not say, 'There are still four months and then comes the harvest'? Behold, I say unto you, Lift up your eyes and look at the fields, for they are already white for harvest! And he who reaps receives wages, and gathers fruit for eternal life, that both he who sows and he who reaps may rejoice together. For in this the saying is true: 'One sows and another reaps.' I sent you to reap that for which you have not laboured; others have laboured, and you have entered into their labours.*
> (John 4:34–38)

Jesus declared that to do God's will and to complete God's work was His food—His nourishment, sustenance and strength. He then went on to describe in vivid terms what the will and work of God was, not only for Himself, but for disciples of all generations: Reaping the harvest of the earth, gathering fruit for eternal life, and proclaiming the salvation of God to all peoples and all nations!

Living and ministering in the will of God releases supernatural strength and power in one's life in all three dimensions: spirit, soul and body.

Power with purpose

Throughout the Bible, living and ministering in the will of God is linked with special manifestations of God's grace—endowments of power, wisdom, strength, knowledge and ability.

For example, in Acts 1:8 Jesus promised His disciples that they would receive supernatural power when the Holy Spirit came upon them; however, that power was inseparably linked to and contingent upon them being Christ's witnesses in Jerusalem, Judea and Samaria, and to the uttermost parts of the earth. As long as they walked in God's will, going everywhere and preaching the Word, the Lord worked with them in mighty power.

God's power is given to us for the express purpose of accomplishing His will. Therefore, we will only see the full release of His power as we learn to live and minister in His will.

God's power works within the framework of God's will. The Apostle Paul illustrated this truth in a much quoted but largely misunderstood verse of Scripture in Philippians 4:13; *'I can do all things through Christ who strengthens me.'*

Some have taken that to mean, 'I can do anything I want to do through Christ.' However, that is a humanistic, self-aggrandising perversion of God's Word.

Paul was in prison in Rome; his life was at stake, pending the verdict of the Imperial Court. He was experiencing deprivation and hardship. Yet in the midst of it all he writes an epistle of joy!

In chapter four he alludes to the various experiences he had been called upon to pass through in the course of serving

Jesus. He knew what it was like to be abased and to suffer need; he also knew what it was like to be full and to abound.

And in verse thirteen he declares, 'I can face any situation that comes to me in the course of God's will for my life, I can do anything God asks me to do in the service of the Lord Jesus, and the secret of my power is that Christ Himself strengthens me!'

Paul could not claim Christ's strength to do something apart from the revealed will of God. God only empowers that which he authorises! If you want to experience the flow of God's power, get into the mainstream of His will.

In the first chapter of the epistle to the Colossians, Paul prays that they may be filled with the knowledge of God's will in all wisdom and spiritual understanding. Such knowledge must be translated into obedient action...walking worthy of the Lord, being fully pleasing to Him, bearing fruit in every good work, increasing in the knowledge of God.

As Paul points out in his classic prayer, knowledge of and obedience to God's will causes us to be *'strengthened with all might according to His glorious power'* (Colossians 1:9–11).

The power of God is manifested when the will of God is known and obeyed. Hence, the will of God is the power of life!

3

The Parameter Of Life

In the Bible, life is likened to a river, whether it be God's eternal life or natural human life (John 7:38 and Proverbs 21:1).

A river has certain significant features that distinguish it from a lake or an ocean. For example, a river FLOWS in a certain direction; it follows a definite COURSE; it has an identifiable BEGINNING and END; and its direction and capacity is controlled to a large extent by BANKS.

Likewise, our life in Christ is intended of God to flow in a certain direction: we are exhorted to press on toward the goal for the prize of the upward call of God in Christ Jesus (Philippians 3:14). We are also called to follow a definite course: the example of Christ, into whose image we are being changed (1 Peter 2:21). Our life in Christ too, has an identifiable beginning (Ephesians 1:13) and a glorious end (1 Thessalonians 4:16,17).

Furthermore, the dimension and direction of our life in Christ is determined by 'banks'—Divinely appointed parameters, those parameters being the revealed will and purpose of God for our life in Christ Jesus.

A river that has no banks ceases to be a river. It becomes a meaningless expanse of water, going nowhere and accomplishing nothing. Likewise, a Christian without Divinely appointed parameters in life and ministry is undisciplined, lawless, and out of control. Consequently, they try to run in every direction at once, be all things to all men and follow every wind of doctrine that blows through the Church.

Such a person has no firm foundation, no fixed direction and no definite goal. They *'sow much, but bring in little'* (Haggai 1:6); they expend much energy but bear little fruit (John 15:2).

The will of God is both restricting and releasing: restricting, in the sense that it narrows our options and ultimately leaves us with only one choice; and releasing, in the sense that God's way and God's way alone will bring complete fulfilment and perfect satisfaction to one's life. *'You will show me the path of life; in Your Presence is fulness of joy; at Your right hand are pleasures forevermore'* (Psalm 16:11).

Jesus referred to both the restriction and the release that God's will brings to one's life, in Matthew 7:13,14:

> *Enter by the narrow gate; for wide is the gate and broad is the way that leads to destruction, and there are many who go in by it. Because narrow is the gate and difficult is the way which leads to life, and there are few who find it.*

Two ways of life are here contrasted. One is wide and spacious, with plenty of room for doing one's own thing. The Bible describes such a person as one who does what is right in his own sight, who is a law unto himself, who fulfils the desires of the flesh and of the mind.

What a life! No one to answer to. No one to please except yourself. No rules to abide by. Absolute freedom! Or is it?

Jesus declared that this way of life would end in nothing less than total destruction! Sin, as Isaiah defines it, is *'going astray, turning to one's own way'* (Isaiah 53:6). And the wages of sin, inevitably, is death (Romans 6:23). Regretfully, the 'many who go by this way' includes both those who outrightly reject the will of God, and others who accept

God's will but try to accomplish it in their own strength and wisdom.

In sharp contrast, Jesus used the word 'narrow' or 'difficult' to describe God's way of life. The Greek word *'thlibo'* literally means 'to press', i.e., to be confined or hemmed in. The word suggests the picture of a narrow road, winding its way through a mountain range, surrounded or 'pressed in' on both sides by towering cliffs.

The will of God is restricting. However, the restriction is for our good. There is only one way that leads to life eternal. There is only one will that can produce righteousness, peace and joy.

The all-wise, all-loving Creator alone knows what is best for His creatures. True freedom and fulfilment can only be found within the confines of God's will. The prophet Jeremiah illustrated this truth in his declaration to Judah:

> *I have not lost sight of My plan for you, the Lord says,*
> *And it is your welfare I have in mind, not your undoing:*
> *for you, too, I have a destiny and a home.*
>
> (Jeremiah 29:11, KNOX)

The great temptation

The first temptation to sin was, in essence, Satan's challenge to man to live independently of God. However, the idyllic dream of freedom and fulfilment through self-determination went horribly wrong. Man found himself eternally separated from God and in bondage to the power of sin. Identified with Satan in his rebellion, man became a prisoner of darkness.

Thank God, Jesus Christ broke the curse through His death on the cross, redeemed us from sin and reconciled us to the Father. But now, having been made alive together with Christ, we must learn to walk in newness of life. Having been set free from sin, we must learn to live in absolute dependence on and complete obedience to the Lord God.

Perhaps the greatest challenge that confronts a born-again, Spirit-filled Christian is the discipline of living within the parameters of God's will.

Every believer needs to learn to abide—to dwell contentedly—within the calling of God upon his or her life (1 Corinthians 7:17,24). God is looking for men and women who are 'under authority'—servants who are conscious of and committed to the will of their Master (Matthew 8:9).

May God grant us grace to abide within the calling with which we have been called, that we may live the rest of our time in the flesh not for the lusts of men, but for THE WILL OF GOD! (1 Peter 4:2).

4

The Seedbed Of Fruitfulness

Most products work best when used for their intended purpose and in accordance with the manufacturer's instructions. How true that is of life, with respect to God's will and human potential!

One can only realise the fullness of his or her God-given potential as one submits to and embraces the will of God for his or her life. Maximum productivity is only possible within the framework of God's revealed will.

Jesus illustrated this principle of truth during His final discourse with the disciples on the night in which He was betrayed. Having concluded the eating of the Passover meal in the upper room, during which time He inaugurated the New Covenant in His own blood, Jesus began to talk to the eleven about the ministry of the Holy Spirit and their role as witnesses of this New Covenant.

> *I am the true vine, and My Father is the vinedresser. Every branch in Me that does not bear fruit He takes away; and every branch that bears fruit He prunes, that it may bear more fruit. You are already clean because of the word which I have spoken to you. Abide in me, and I in you. As the branch cannot bear fruit of itself, unless it abides in the vine, neither can you, unless you abide in Me. I am the vine, you are the branches. He who abides in Me, and I in Him, bears much fruit; for without Me you can do nothing. If anyone does not abide in Me, He*

is cast out as a branch and is withered; and they gather them and throw them into the fire, and they are burned. If you abide in Me, and My words abide in you, you will ask what you desire, and it shall be done for you. By this My Father is glorified, that you bear much fruit; so you will be My disciples. (John 15:1–8)

Jesus made it very clear that the Father looks for fruitfulness in the lives of His children. Jesus also spoke of various levels of degrees of fruitfulness—'fruit', 'more fruit' and 'much fruit'. The degree of fruitfulness in one's life is commensurate with the degree to which one abides in Christ.

What does it mean to 'abide in Christ'? The Amplified Bible translates it this way: *'To abide vitally united to Christ'*. Obviously, the word 'abide' speaks of a deep, living union with the Lord Jesus Christ, made gloriously possible through the miracle of the New Birth and the Baptism of the Holy Spirit.

It also indicates an ongoing relationship, a day to day fellowship, and an intimate communion with the Lord, in which we partake of His life and nature and thereby bear the fruit of His Spirit.

The word 'abide' introduces us to a life of prayer and worship, walking in the Spirit, meditation in the Word, waiting on the Lord and a dynamic sharing of His resurrection power.

However, 'abiding in Christ' has an even greater scope of meaning than this. To 'abide in Christ' is to live under Christ's Lordship; to be governed and controlled by His Word and His Spirit; to do His will and not our own; to fulfil His plan and purpose in the time allotted to us on earth.

This kind of intimate communion with the Lord and joyful submission and wholehearted dedication to His will becomes the seedbed of fruitfulness in life and ministry.

Fruitfulness in and by the will of God

The Apostle Paul was ever conscious of the absolute importance of being in the will of God and of being led by the Spirit as he sought to fulfil the calling of God upon his life. He recognised that the full blessing of Christ would only be manifested in his life and ministry as he moved in conjunction with the power of the Holy Spirit and in accordance with the will of God.

> *For God is my witness, whom I serve with my spirit in the Gospel of His Son, that without ceasing I make mention of you always in my prayers, Making request if, by some means, now at last I may find a way IN THE WILL OF GOD to come to you. For I long to see you, that I may impart to you some spiritual gift, so that you may be established—That is, that I may be encouraged together with you by the mutual faith of you and me. Now I do not want you to be unaware, brethren, that I often planned to come to you (but was hindered until now), that I might have some fruit among you also, just as among the other Gentiles.* (Romans 1:9–13)

In the fifteenth chapter of Romans Paul continues with this same theme of ministering in the power of the Spirit and in the will of God:

> *But I know that when I come to you, I shall come in the fullness of the blessing of the Gospel of Christ. Now I beg you, brethren, through the Lord Jesus Christ, and through the love of the Spirit, that you strive together with me in your prayers to God for me, That I may be delivered from those in Judea who do not believe, and that my service for Jerusalem may be acceptable to the saints, That I may come to you with joy BY THE WILL*

OF GOD, and may be refreshed together with you.
(Romans 15:29–32)

The anointing of God upon Paul's life functioned so long as he faithfully stayed within the parameters of God's will. One of the grave dangers of exceeding the Word of the Lord and venturing into spheres and places of ministry where God has not called us is the potential of being deceived and inheriting a false anointing.

We must not presume on the grace or the gifting of God. God is with us so long as we are with Him in the place of his appointment. God says to us, *'I will set your boundaries...'* (Exodus 23:31) and *'I will appoint a place for My people Israel, and will plant them'* (2 Samuel 7:10). But if we wilfully step over our God-appointed boundaries and move outside our God-ordained sphere of ministry we will find ourselves 'running in the flesh' without the Spirit of the Lord.

If we persist in our own way we will find ourselves both deceiving and being deceived. Such a ministry will only produce 'Ishmaels'—sons of the flesh. It will never please God or accomplish His purpose.

Fruitfulness that glorifies God

It is of critical importance that we both hear and obey the voice of the Holy Spirit as He seeds to lead us into the will and purpose of God. Like Paul, our fruitfulness in life and ministry depends on it!

Paul's desire was that he might impart a spiritual gift to the saints so as to establish them in the faith; that he might be encouraged together with them by their mutual faith; that he might have some fruit among them through the preaching of the Gospel and the demonstration of the power of God; that he might come to them with joy and be refreshed together with them—that the fullness of the blessing of the

Gospel of Christ might be manifested as he ministered among them!

But Paul, in humility and wisdom, acknowledged that the key to all these things was his being there in the will of God, and to that end he requested the saints to pray for him.

The bottom line of fruitfulness is not 'our' gifts, talents or ability—it is abiding in Christ and being in the will of God. Christians who learn to live, move and have their being in the will of God bear lasting fruit and thereby glorify the Name of the Lord in the earth!

5

An Attitude

One often thinks of the will of God as being circumstantial; that is, being in the right place at the right time. As we will discover in our study, this is certainly true. However, the will of God encompasses much more than just events and appointments.

The Bible teaches us that the will of God is firstly AN ATTITUDE. In fact, throughout the Bible God deals with attitudes before He deals with behaviour, because in the final analysis, one's attitude dictates one's behaviour.

The classic teaching of our Lord on the Kingdom of God, often referred to as 'The Beatitudes' or 'The sermon on the mount' is a case in point. Jesus spoke about attitudes of humility, Godly sorrow, meekness, righteousness, mercy, purity, restoration and endurance, and then declared that these attitudes would cause us to behave in such a way that we would be as salt to the earth and light to the world! Men would see the good works that proceeded from our Christ-like character and would glorify our Father in heaven! (Matthew 5:3–16).

Truth in the inward parts

It is possible to have the right truth but the wrong spirit. It is also possible to be doing the right thing with the wrong attitude. In seeking to discover and define the will of God for our lives it is important to start where God starts, and that is with the attitudes of the heart.

Jesus put the emphasis where it belonged when He declared to His disciples:

> *But those things which proceed out of the mouth come from the heart, and they defile a man. For out of the heart proceed evil thoughts, murders, adulteries, fornications, thefts, false witness, blasphemies.*
> (Matthew 15:18,19)

God desires truth in our inward parts (Psalm 51:6). His will is that the character of Christ be formed in us (Galatians 4:19); that we be partakers of His Divine nature (2 Peter 1:4); that the attitudes which characterised the life of Jesus may be in us and may dictate our behaviour (Philippians 2:1–16).

King David was very aware of God's dealings in his life and of his need for spiritual renewal and attitude adjustment. The cry of his heart was,

> *Create in me a clean heart, O God, and renew a steadfast spirit within me.* (Psalm 51:10)

> *Search me, O God, and know my heart: try me, and know my thoughts: And see if there be any wicked way in me, and lead me in the way everlasting.*
> (Psalm 139:23,24, KJV)

The will of God for our lives is that we be conformed to the image of His Son, Jesus Christ, that He might be the firstborn among many brethren (Romans 8:29). We are called to be like Jesus in both character and conduct.

We are to *'let this attitude be in us which was also in Christ Jesus'* (Philippians 2:5) and we are to *'walk in love, as Christ also has loved us and given Himself for us'* (Ephesians 5:2).

We are to *'follow His example'* and *'do the works He has done'* (John 13:15 & 14:2).

The Apostle Paul clearly defined the will of God as being a Christ-like attitude:

> *In everything give thanks; for this is the will of God in Christ Jesus for you.* (1 Thessalonians 5:18)

Thanksgiving and praise; humility and servanthood; faith and perseverance; selflessness and compassion; utter consecration to the Heavenly Father. These were the attitudes which characterised the life and ministry of Jesus. And it is these self-same attitudes which constitute the will of God for our lives, today!

6

A Time And A Place

One can only marvel at the greatness of our God: at His precise planning, His perfect timing, His awesome power and His infinite wisdom. Whether it be the natural creation, with its celestial glory and terrestrial splendour, or the spiritual creation—men and women, redeemed and justified by the blood of the Lamb, and recreated in the image of God in righteousness and true holiness... one can only stand in awe and exclaim, 'My God, how great Thou art!'

With intricate detail and pin-point accuracy our God designed and created the heavens and the earth; He measured the waters in the hollow of His hand and measured heaven with a span; He calculated the dust of the earth in a measure and weighed the mountains in scales and the hills in a balance! (Isaiah 40:12). He numbered the stars and called them all by name! (Psalm 147:4).

Likewise, with infinite wisdom our God conceived and executed the plan of redemption to deliver man from the power of sin and reconcile him unto Himself in righteousness. The Bible declares that the wisdom of God in redemption was so beyond the comprehension of men and angels that none of the rulers of this age (spiritual or natural) could grasp it. And indeed, if they had understood God's plan, they would not have crucified the Lord of Glory! (1 Corinthians 2:7,8).

Whichever way you look at it, our God is an immaculate

Creator and a Master of strategy and implementation. No wonder Paul cried out in adoration and amazement:

> *Oh, the depth of the riches both of the wisdom and knowledge of God! How unsearchable are His judgments and His ways past finding out!* (Romans 11:33)

As we come to appreciate the scope of God's wisdom and the extent of God's power as revealed in His creative and redemptive acts, we can understand what a simple matter it is for God to plan and direct our lives!

The Bible declares that God knows the end from the beginning (Isaiah 46:10). How easy it is then for Him to number our days, prepare our ways and guide our steps!

The Psalmist David described God's ability to lead and guide his people with the same kind of exactness and precision with which he created and continues to sustain the universe:

> *The steps of a good man are ordered by the Lord, and He delights in His way. Though he fall, he shall not be utterly cast down; for the Lord upholds him with His hand.* (Psalm 37:23,24)

The Hebrew word 'kuwn', translated 'to order', has a variety of meanings which will help to enlarge our understanding and appreciation of God's providence. 'Kuwn' means 'to establish, to render sure, proper or prosperous.' It also means 'to direct, to ordain and to order.' Moreover, it carries a sense of Divine 'provision and preparation.' Such is the commitment of God to care for and guide His children, even in the smallest details of life!

Being led by the Spirit

The will of God has to do with a time and a place. God's plan extends to and includes our daily lives—where we are to go, what we are to do, who we are to meet and what we are to say.

If, like Anna of old, we learn the secret of *'not departing from the Temple'*—of abiding in the Presence of God—and *'serving God with fastings and prayers',* we too will *'come in that precise moment'* to witness the Glory of the Lord and to do His will! (Luke 2:36-38).

The secret of being in the right place at the right time to do God's will does not lie in our ability or cleverness, but rather in the ministry of the Holy Spirit who has come to guide us into all truth. If we will learn to rely on the Spirit, yield to the Spirit and obey the Spirit, the will of God will become for us a moment-by-moment reality.

The Holy Spirit progressively leads us into the fullness of the Father's plan and purpose for our lives. The Spirit makes intercession for the saints according to the will of God (Romans 8:27), and it is the Spirit who reveals to us the things that are freely given to us by God (1 Corinthians 2:10,12). We must come into a new dimension of dependence on and obedience to the Spirit if we are going to discover and fulfil the will of God in our lives.

An appointment in Macedonia

On one occasion, as the Apostle Paul was seeking to know the will of God concerning the timing and placement of his ministry, the Holy Spirit forbade him to preach in Asia. Then, when he sought to enter Bythinia, the Spirit again prevented him.

But shortly afterwards, the Spirit gave Paul a vision of a man from Macedonia pleading for him to come over and help them. Concluding that this was the will of God, Paul and his friends set sail for Macedonia and commenced ministry in Philippi.

Little did they know that this was to be a strategic turning point in world missions that would forever alter the course of history! It was the beginning of the spreading of the Gospel in Europe! (Acts 16:6–10). It pays to obey God!

As for God, His ways are perfect. God knows and has already prepared just the right time and place for every purpose under heaven.

We can rest in the assurance that the One who set the stars in their orbital paths, who foreordained the life-span and territorial boundaries of the nations, has a will for our lives that encompasses every day, every decision and every dilemma that we face.

7

A Sphere

'Are all apostles?' asked Paul. *'Are all prophets? Are all teachers? Are all workers of miracles? Do all have gifts of healings? Do all speak with tongues? Do all interpret?'* (1 Corinthians 12:29,30).

The obvious answer is 'No'. As believers in the Lord Jesus Christ, we are all baptised into one body. Although the Church is made up of many individual members, each with different gifts and callings, yet through the unity of the Spirit we are one body, called to glorify God with one mind and one voice.

If we are to grow up spiritually into the image of the Lord Jesus, it is essential that we come to recognise our identity as believers in Christ and our place of membership in His body, the Church.

No man can live unto himself and no man is complete in himself. God has structured life in such a way so as to make us inter-dependent. *'For we, being many, are one bread and one body; for we all partake of that one bread'* (1 Corinthians 10:17). None of us, on our own, constitute the 'whole loaf'.

God's agent

The Church is the instrument of God's revelation to the nations—the agent of His wisdom and power (Ephesians 3:10). The Church is the manifestation of the fullness of

Christ in the earth—the vehicle through which God reveals His glory to the world (Ephesians 1:23).

For this to effectively take place, the Church must come together as a unified body, with each member understanding and fulfilling their God-appointed function. The potential of the Church as the Agent of God is enormous. But the cost of realising that potential is equally as great (Ephesians 4:11–16).

Placement in the body

The will of God for one's life is that sphere of ministry for which one has been equipped by the grace of God. To each one God has allotted a deposit of grace—special gifts and abilities—in accordance with his will and purpose.

On two occasions the Apostle Paul described the will of God as being the unique sphere, role or function assigned by God to each member of the Body of Christ:

> *Now there are diversities of gifts, but the same Spirit. There are differences of ministries, but the same Lord. And there are diversities of activities, but it is the same God who works all in all. But the manifestation of the Spirit is given to each one for the profit of all. But one and the same Spirit works all these things, distributing to each one individually AS HE WILLS. But now God has set the members, each one of them, in the body JUST AS HE PLEASED. And God has appointed these in the Church...* (1 Corinthians 12:4–7,11,18,28)

Please note that the initiative rests exclusively with God. He is Sovereign over His Church. When He calls us He does not give us a list of options. He is not the God of 'multiple choice'. God has only one will and one purpose for each member of the Body. Our only 'choice' is to obey or disobey God's call—to accept or reject His good will.

> *And do not be conformed to this world, but be transformed by the renewing of your mind, that you may prove what is that GOOD AND ACCEPTABLE AND PERFECT WILL OF GOD. For I say, through the grace given to me, to everyone who is among you, not to think of himself more highly than he ought to think, but to think soberly, as God has dealt to each one a measure of faith. For as we have many members in one body, but all the members do not have the same function, So we, being many, are one body in Christ, and individually members of one another. Having then gifts differing according to the grace that is given to us, let us use them...* (Romans 12:2–6)

Once again, the will of God for one's life is spoken of in terms of one's God-appointed place and function in the Body of Christ.

If we, as individuals, and as the corporate Body of Christ, are going to attain the kind of spiritual maturity God is requiring of us in these last days, we must have a revelation of the grace that is given to us in Christ Jesus.

Perception of this grace produces self-acceptance and acceptance of others. It was when James, Peter and John perceived the grace that had been given to Paul that they extended to him and Barnabas the right hand of fellowship (Galatians 2:9).

God desires to enlarge our capacity to recognise and acknowledge the diversities of gifts, the differences of ministries and the diversities of activities that come from His hand.

In the light of the revelation of God's grace, we can 'think soberly', both of ourselves and others. To 'think soberly' means to 'think reasonably of one's self' or to 'have a sane estimate of one's capabilities'. Conceit is actually a form of insanity!

A measure of faith

God deals to each member of Christ's Body a 'measure of faith'. That 'measure of faith' is essentially 'functioning faith', and should not be confused with the gift of 'saving faith' mentioned in Ephesians 2:8. The measure of faith varies from person to person and is in accordance with the will and purpose of God for one's life.

For example, if God calls you to be an evangelist, He will give you faith to function as an evangelist. One's spiritual gift or grace operates in proportion to one's measure of faith. One's measure of faith will certainly increase as one walks in obedience to the revelation of God, thereby enlarging the sphere and increasing the fruitfulness of one's ministry.

However, the measure of faith is limited to the calling and gifting of God in one's life. With the calling to be an evangelist comes the faith to fulfil the ministry of an evangelist. But such a measure of faith would not extend to the ministry of a pastor or teacher, if that ministry was not part of God's calling upon your life.

Working within the limits of your sphere

It is so important, both for our own sake and for the sake of the Church at large, that we learn to function within the sphere of ministry which God has appointed us. It is also important that we recognise and accept the limits of our God-appointed sphere and do not try to extend ourselves into another man's area of ministry. The Word of God makes it clear that if we are faithful in doing what God has called us to do, He will not only reward us but will also enlarge our sphere and increase our measure!

> *For we dare not class ourselves or compare ourselves with those who commend themselves. But they, measuring themselves by themselves, and comparing themselves among themselves, are not wise. We, however, will not boast beyond measure, but within the limits of the sphere which God appointed us—a sphere which especially includes you. For we are not extending ourselves beyond our sphere (thus not reaching you), for it was to you that we came with the Gospel of Christ; Not boasting of things beyond measure, that is, in other men's labors, but having hope, that as your faith is increased, we shall be greatly enlarged by you in our sphere, To preach the Gospel in the regions beyond you, and not to boast in another man's sphere of accomplishment.*
> (2 Corinthians 10:12–16)

Do you know what it will take to reach the world for Jesus in our generation? Simply this: every believer, fulfilling the will of God in his or her life. Doing what God has called them to do. Discovering their place in the Body of Christ and ministering in their God-appointed sphere.

This would not only bring the Body of Christ to full stature, but would also turn the world upside down with a manifestation of the power of God, hitherto unknown in our generation!

8

A Dedicated Life

The Bible reveals two primary conditions for knowing God's will. They are found in the twelfth chapter of Romans, verses one and 2:

> *I beseech you therefore, brethren, by the mercies of God, that you present your bodies a living sacrifice, holy, acceptable to God, which is your reasonable service. And do not be conformed to this world, but be transformed by the renewing of your mind, that you may prove what is that good and acceptable and perfect will of God.*

In this chapter we will consider the first condition for knowing God's will: A DEDICATED LIFE.

The Word of God exhorts us that in view of and on the basis of the mercies of God, we ought to present our bodies as living sacrifices unto Him. In fact, a wholehearted dedication of one's life to God is the only appropriate response one could make to the great mercy God has extended to us through Jesus Christ.

This 'living sacrifice' is to be presented in the same vein as the 'whole burnt offering' of the Old Covenant (Leviticus 1). It belongs entirely to God—every part is presented to Him. And it is consumed entirely by fire, symbolising the complete sanctification of the sacrifice and its full acceptance by God.

Likewise, our lives (spirit, soul and body) are to be offered to God as spiritual sacrifices. We ought not to hold back any part, but rather, dedicate ourselves wholeheartedly and completely to Him. And in response, the Spirit of God will fill our lives with the Presence and Power of God, thereby setting us apart in holiness unto the Lord. and it is through the precious blood of Jesus, His finished work on the Cross, and the sanctifying power of the Spirit that we are made acceptable to God!

Such wholehearted dedication qualifies one for the knowledge of God's will. The Bible teaches us that the Lord God does not share His secrets with just anyone; He does not disseminate his knowledge anywhere and everywhere.

Rather, *'the secret of the Lord is with those who fear Him, and He will show them His covenant'* (Psalm 25:14). God says, *'You will seek Me and find Me, when you search for Me with all your heart'* (Jeremiah 29:13). And furthermore, *'Draw near to God, and He will draw near to you'* (James 4:8).

Jesus highlighted the principle of qualifying for the knowledge of God's will through spiritual desire and dedication as He taught in the temple during the Feast of Tabernacles:

> *Now about the middle of the Feast Jesus went up into the temple and taught. And the Jews marvelled, saying, 'How does this man know letters, having never studied?' Jesus answered them and said, 'My doctrine is not Mine, but His who sent Me. IF ANYONE WANTS TO DO HIS WILL, HE SHALL KNOW CONCERNING THE DOCTRINE, whether it is from God or whether I speak on My own authority'.* (John 7:14–17)

Everything Jesus knew, He knew by the revelation of the Spirit of God. And He qualified for the revelation knowledge through an unreserved dedication of His life to the will of God. From the first moments of adolescence until His appearance in the temple He had committed Himself to be about *'His Father's business'* (Luke 2:49).

Jesus was totally identified with the Father; He was totally committed to the Father. As a result, He could say, *'My doctrine is not Mine, but His who sent Me... The Father loves the Son and shows Him all things that He Himself does... I am in the Father, and the Father in Me. The words that I speak to you I do not speak on My own authority; but the Father who dwells in Me does the works.'*

And with these eager and astonished listeners in the temple, Jesus shares the key to the knowledge of God: 'If anyone WANTS TO DO HIS WILL, he shall know concerning the doctrine...!'

The first step in proving what is that good, acceptable and perfect will of God is to present our bodies as living sacrifices, holy and well-pleasing to God, which is our spiritual and intelligent service of worship.

Unless we make this commitment, we will never leave first base in our quest for the knowledge of God. There are no shortcuts, there are no alternative routes. The Fear of the Lord is the beginning of wisdom. Dedication to God is the beginning of revelation knowledge.

9

A Renewed Mind

The second prerequisite for knowing God's will is A RENEWED MIND. The Word of God exhorts us:

> *And do not be conformed to this world, but be transformed by the renewing of your mind, that you may prove what is that good and acceptable and perfect will of God.* (Romans 12:2)

It is important to remember that the Apostle Paul is writing to Christians in Rome, not unbelievers, to the end that they might grow up spiritually into the image of Jesus Christ and prove experientially the good, acceptable and perfect will of God. In other words, that they might become all that God intends them to be as new creatures in Christ Jesus.

The great danger that confronts all Christians is conformity to the world through compromise. Having dedicated ourselves to God (verse one), we now find our commitment being challenged by the 'spirit of this world'. If we are going to press on and lay hold of that for which Christ has laid hold of us, if we are going to know and fulfil the will of God in our lives, we will have to pass this test and overcome the temptation to conform.

> *Do not love the world or the things in the world. If anyone loves the world, the love of the Father is not in*

> *him. For all that is in the world—the lust of the flesh, the lust of the eyes, and the pride of life—is not of the Father but is of the world. And the world is passing away, and the lust of it; but he who does the will of God abides forever.* (1 John 2:15–17)

Christians are called to a lifestyle of repentance. We are to be continually turning away from sin and turning to God; continually and increasingly turning away from the lusts of the flesh and embracing the righteousness of God.

True repentance is a gift of God—we cannot achieve it on our own (2 Timothy 2:25). It is the goodness of God, manifested in the conviction of the Holy Spirit that leads us to repentance (Romans 2:4).

If we are sensitive to the ministry of the Holy Spirit, we will find that He is continually impelling us to separate ourselves from the world and to separate ourselves unto the will and purpose of God. What a debt we owe to the faithfulness of the Holy Spirit!

One cannot love God and love the world. One cannot walk in both light and darkness at the same time. Purity of heart and holiness of life are prerequisites for seeing God (Matthew 5:8 & Hebrews 12:14). One cannot know God or His will 'from afar'. To enter into the knowledge of God we must be crucified to the world and the world to us. Separation from the world leads to intimacy with the Father.

> *Therefore come out from among them and be separate, says the Lord. Do not touch what is unclean, and I will receive you. I will be a Father to you, and you shall be My sons and daughters, says the Lord Almighty. Therefore, having these promises, beloved, let us cleanse ourselves from all filthiness of the flesh and spirit, perfecting holiness in the fear of God.*
> (2 Corinthians 6:17,18 & 7:1)

The key to transformation

The Bible reveals the key to separation from the world and transformation into the image of Christ. It is called, *'The Renewing of the Mind'*. Your mind is the key to your life. *'As a man thinks in his heart, so is he'*, declared the writer of Proverbs (Proverbs 23:7).

The mind is the great battlefield of life. Your behaviour is dictated by your thinking patterns and attitudes. If you can change your mind, you can change your whole life! This is the reason why the Bible places such emphasis on 'renewing the mind' with the truth of God's Word.

The renewing of the mind (Gk: *'anakainosis'*) means to 'renew, renovate and completely change for the better.' It also holds the thought of 'the restoration of the image of God.' It signifies a complete change of attitude, a whole new set of ideals, a totally new perspective and a completely different focus and pattern of thinking. The word indicates an ongoing process of renewal, which, in turn, initiates an ongoing process of transformation in one's life.

Our minds need to be renewed because through the fall they became darkened...set on the flesh and the things of this world...blinded by the god of this age.

In Isaiah 55:8,9 God says,

> *For My thoughts are not your thoughts, nor are your ways My ways, for as the heavens are higher than the earth, so are My ways higher than your ways, and My thoughts than your thoughts.*

However, this incompatibility was never God's intention, nor was it the case when God first created man. God created Adam with a spirit that was perfectly in tune with His own Spirit and a mind that was perfectly in tune with His own Mind. Adam's mind was filled with the thoughts of God— creative thoughts, holy thoughts, pure thoughts, powerful thoughts. No wonder he was able to give to each animal a name that perfectly reflects its unique character and ability!

God's redemptive purpose in Christ is to renew our thought patterns and attitudes so that they reflect the thoughts and attitudes of His own heart and mind. However, this is a life-long process and is only as effective as our co-operation with the Holy Spirit, by Whose power we are changed into the image of Christ from glory to glory! (2 Corinthians 3:18).

One reason why many Christians fail to prove what is that good, acceptable and perfect will of God is that they approach God and His Word with carnal, unrenewed minds. They rationalise truth and fail to discern the voice of the Spirit because their minds are set on the things of the flesh. Such an approach will never succeed because *'the carnal mind is enmity against God'* and *'to be carnally minded is death, but to be spiritually minded is life and peace'* (Romans 8:6,7).

Developing a spiritual mind-set

How then does one become 'spiritually-minded'? How does the process of renewal work?

First of all, the Bible tells us to 'SET OUR MINDS' on the things of God.

> *If then you were raised with Christ, seek those things which are above, where Christ is, sitting at the right hand of God. Set your mind on things above, not on things on the earth. For you died, and your life is hidden with Christ in God.* (Colossians 3:1–3)

The Christian is to have a mind-set that is Heavenly, eternal and spiritual—centred on God and His Word. This is achieved principally through meditation in the Word and prayer.

> *This Book of the Law shall not depart from your mouth, but you shall meditate in it day and night, that you may observe to do according to all that is written in it. For then you will make your way prosperous, and then you will have good success.* (Joshua 1:8)

The Word judges and purifies our motives; it transforms our attitudes and goals to be like those of Christ Himself. As we meditate in the Word our minds are filled with the thoughts of God. Light and Life are imparted to our spirits. Our lives begin to open up in the Presence of God. The Holy Spirit is able to speak to our hearts and reveal secrets of eternal truth.

Meditation in the Word moves us into a position where we can prove what is that good and acceptable and perfect will of God, and in so doing, make our way prosperous and have good success, to the glory of God!

Praying in the Spirit

The second factor in the renewal of the mind is 'PRAYING IN THE SPIRIT'. There is a world of difference between mere 'prayer' and 'praying in the Spirit'. As Christians, we are called not just to pray, but to *'pray at all times, with all kinds of prayer, in the power of the Spirit'* (Ephesians 6:18). In other words, we are to pray Spirit-inspired and Spirit-energised prayers. We are to be vehicles for the Spirit's intercession. The Holy Spirit knows the will of God perfectly, and as we pray He guides us into the knowledge and fulfilment of that will.

> *Likewise the Spirit also helps in our weaknesses. For we*

> *do not know what we should pray for as we ought, but the Spirit Himself makes intercession for us with groanings which cannot be uttered. Now He who searches the hearts knows what the mind of the Spirit is, because He makes intercession for the saints according to the will of God.* (Romans 8:26,27)

The Apostle Paul also speaks of the revelation of God's will that comes through praying in the Spirit:

> *For this reason we also, since the day we heard it, do not cease to pray for you, and to ask that you may be filled with the knowledge of His will in all wisdom and spiritual understanding; That you may have a walk worthy of the Lord, fully pleasing Him, being fruitful in every good work and increasing in the knowledge of God.* (Colossians 1:9,10)

The word 'knowledge' denotes 'exact knowledge' or 'full knowledge' or 'clear knowledge'. Praise God that it is possible to have an exact, full, deep and clear knowledge of His will in all wisdom and spiritual understanding!

One aspect of Spirit-filled praying that is worthy of special consideration is 'praying in other tongues' or 'glossolalia'.

In the Book of Acts, 'speaking in tongues' was the initial evidence or expression of the Baptism of the Holy Spirit. On the Day of Pentecost, when the Holy Spirit fell on the 120 disciples gathered in the upper room, they praised and magnified God in languages which they did not know (Acts 2). Down through church history, 'tongues' has continued to be an outstanding feature of the outpouring of the Holy Spirit.

However, 'tongues' is not intended of God to be touted about as a badge of spiritual superiority (as some have done); rather, it is a passport into the supernatural realm of the Holy Spirit. It is a tool of spiritual warfare. It is a gift for edifying the Church (when accompanied by interpretation).

But most of all, it is a means of communication for ministering unto God in thanksgiving, praise, worship and intercession.

As the Apostle Paul points out, when it comes to prayer, our understanding is extremely limited. Many times we know that we need to pray, but we don't know how to pray or what to pray for. And it is to this end that God has ordained 'glossolalia' as an aid in prayer and worship.

Speaking in tongues bridges the gap between the natural and the supernatural—it causes us to move from the realm of the flesh into the realm of the Spirit. Speaking in tongues sensitises one's spirit to the Voice and Presence of the Holy Spirit and focuses one's mind on things above. Speaking in tongues moves us into a place where we can hear from God and receive revelation of His will for our lives.

As we learn to wait on the Lord and minister to Him in spiritual languages, we will find the interpretation of our prayer coming back to us from the Holy Spirit, thereby renewing our minds and enlarging our understanding of God's purpose. Like Paul, we will pray with the Spirit and with the understanding, and walk in the light of God's revealed will (1 Corinthians 14:15).

Prayer and fasting

Another factor in the process of renewal which, when combined with prayer, has a powerful effect on our lives and helps to facilitate the fulfilment of God's will, is 'FASTING'.

> *Then I proclaimed a fast there at the river of Ahava, that we might humble ourselves before our God, to seek from Him the right way for us and our little ones and all our possessions.* (Ezra 8:21)

Fasting has an important part to play in the outworking of

the plans and purposes of God. When God puts you on a fast it will invariably lead to a stripping away of the flesh and a humbling of your soul before Him. This in turn, will pave the way for an increased dimension of God's anointing and revelation in your life!

Prayer and fasting should be a way of life for the Christian. However, there are times when we have to devote ourselves to special concentrated periods of prayer and fasting, in order to see a breakthrough in the situation that confronts us. Sometimes, it is **THE ONLY WAY** to move forward in the will of God!

10

The Value Of Godly Counsel

'Blessed is the man who walks not in the counsel of the ungodly' declared the Psalmist (Psalm 1:1). Unfortunately, some Christians have taken it to mean, 'Blessed is the man who does not walk in counsel,' and have acted accordingly!

The Bible does not warn us to avoid counsel, but rather to avoid UNGODLY COUNSEL. In fact, we are exhorted to seek out and walk in the counsel of Godly men and women of proven character.

> *Where there is no counsel, the people fall; But in the multitude of counsellors there is safety.* (Proverbs 11:14)

As we have already noted in chapter 7, no man can live unto himself. God structured life in such a way so as to make us dependent on one another. *'God sets the solitary in families, He brings out those who are bound into prosperity; but the rebellious dwell in a dry land'* (Psalm 68:6).

God intends for every believer to be part of a New Testament structured local church, and to share in all the benefits and responsibilities of a spiritual family.

The role of shepherds

One of the benefits of congregational life is the oversight and care of Godly men and women who function as shepherds of the flock of God.

Every Christian needs a pastor. However, just attending a church and listening to someone preach does not necessarily make that person your pastor. Regretfully, there are many 'shepherd-less' people in the Body of Christ today. 'Sheep without a shepherd' inevitably become harassed, distressed and confused (Matthew 9:36).

The Bible gives us clear instruction on how to relate to those who are over us in the Lord, whom God has appointed as shepherds and teachers in the local assembly.

> *Remember those who rule over you, who have spoken the Word of God to you, whose faith follow, considering the outcome of their conduct. Obey those who rule over you, and be submissive, for they watch out for your souls, as those who must give account. Let them do so with joy and not with grief, for that would be unprofitable for you.* (Hebrews 13:7,17)

If they are men and women of proven character, and if they are teaching the true Word of God, we should follow them as they follow Christ.

A faithful shepherd watches out for the souls of his flock. He teaches them the Way of the Lord; he imparts wisdom and knowledge; he prays, he warns, he encourages, he corrects. If the sheep are submissive and obedient, they will be preserved from evil and will prosper in the will of God. But if they are self-willed and rebellious, they will *'dwell in a dry land'*—they will die in the wilderness, outside of God's purpose and inheritance.

If we are going to prove what is that good, acceptable and perfect will of God, we must walk in the counsel of the faithful men and women whom God has appointed to watch over us in Christ.

Isolationism often leads to extremism or error. There is

safety in numbers, when those numbers represent the holy remnant of God's people. Learn to walk in relationship with the members of the spiritual family in which God has placed you. Learn to submit yourself to the watch-care of your spiritual leaders. Seek their advice. Listen to their counsel. Hear the Word of the Lord from their lips.

The bronze altar

One of the obstacles to receiving the knowledge of God's will is 'self-will'. We come to God full of plans, ideas, desires and ambitions, and expect Him to bless them. God cannot fill us with the knowledge of HIS WILL unless we are emptied of self-will!

The layout of the Tabernacle of Moses typifies our approach to the Presence of God. Before the priest ever reached the Holy Place containing the Table of Shewbread, the Lampstand and the Golden Altar, he first had to visit the Bronze Altar and the Laver of Cleansing.

The Bronze Altar with its sacrificial offerings and shedding of blood represents the Cross of our Lord Jesus Christ. The first station on our journey into the Presence of God to discover His will for our lives is the Cross!

It is on the Cross that our self-life is crucified with Christ. It is on the Cross that we yield our will to the will of the Father.

The fact that many people avoid the 'Bronze Altar' (the Cross) on their way into the Presence of God is evidenced by their unwillingness to submit to their pastors, who represent Christ's authority in the local church.

In my years of ministry I have found that, generally speaking, people are more inclined to make decisions WITHOUT consulting the prayerful counsel of their pastor. The reason for this, in many cases, is that people are not sure that what they are proposing to do is the will of God, and they are afraid that if they submit it to their pastor he might say 'No!'

Such an attitude betrays the fact that our commitment is not to the will of God, but to our own will. If that is the case, we had better return to the Bronze Altar (the Cross), and get our priorities right!

Do not be afraid of the men and women whom God has given to lead you. They are an indispensable part of God's programme to change you into the image of Jesus Christ!

'Blessed is the man who walks in the counsel of the Godly...'

11

How To Discern The Will Of God

The Book of Acts is a record of men and women being empowered by the Holy Spirit to do the works of Jesus. It is the Divine standard and pattern for all people of all generations.

I appreciate the candidness of the record, and in particular, its unashamed portrayal of the struggles of the apostles and the Early Church to come to grips with the will of God.

At times the Spirit's leading was very clear; the Word of the Lord resounded like a trumpet; the Church acted promptly and decisively in the will of God. At other times their vision was somewhat blurred; they were slow to understand and slow to respond—in fact, on more than one occasion they needed some extra motivation in the form of persecution to galvanise them into action!

On certain occasions it took time for them to see the issues clearly; they had to overcome natural prejudices, misconceptions and erroneous expectations. Sometimes it took much prayer and seeking of God to really know His will, perceive His purpose and understand His plan. At other times it took the direct intervention of God in Divinely ordered circumstances to change their perspective and direction. I can identify with all of this!

Revelation and relationship

Knowing the will of God is no simple matter. It cannot be

reduced to a mere formula or a series of steps. Knowing the will of God is part of knowing God Himself, and that kind of knowledge only comes by REVELATION, and revelation comes as we build RELATIONSHIP.

Building a relationship with God is the single most important thing anyone can do in this life. Developing a deep and meaningful relationship with God demands the best of our time, strength and resources. However, the amount of time we spend in prayer and meditation in the Word of God will be directly reflected in the degree to which we know God and understand His will for our lives. 'Knowing God' is the supreme goal of life. More than anything else, it is the true measure of success and failure.

> *Thus says the Lord: 'Let not the wise man glory in his wisdom, Let not the mighty man glory in his might, Nor let the rich man glory in his riches; But let him who glories glory in this, That he understands and knows Me, That I am the LORD, exercising loving kindness, judgment, and righteousness in the earth. For in these I delight,' says the LORD.* (Jeremiah 9:23,24)

The three witnesses

There are three primary witnesses that confirm the will of God in our lives: The Word, the Spirit, and the Providence of God. These three work together in agreement and help to chart a clear course in the will of God. In this chapter we will consider the first of these witnesses:

The Word

God's Word IS His will. There is no higher authority in

heaven or on earth than the Word of God. If God has said it, that forever settles it. God's Word is the revelation of His will and purpose. It is His covenant—His immutable and eternal commitment, ratified by the Blood of the Lord Jesus Christ.

In our quest to know the will of God, the Bible should always be our first point of reference and our final court of appeal. We need to prioritise the written Word of God, realising that it is indeed, 'God breathed'.

> *All scripture is given by inspiration of God, and is profitable for doctrine, for reproof, for correction, for instruction in righteousness, That the man of God may be complete, thoroughly equipped for every good work.*
> (2 Timothy 3:16,17)

The Word of God is profitable! The Word of God teaches us the Way of the Lord and instructs us in the paths of righteousness. If we give heed to it, it will direct our steps into the will of God and establish our feet on a sure foundation.

The Word exposes secret sins and hidden flaws; it judges the thoughts and intents of the heart. It corrects the error of our way, thereby saving us from destruction and a multitude of sins.

If we allow the Word to do its work by giving it first place in our lives, submitting to its Lordship and obeying its voice, it will mature us into the image of Jesus Christ and will thoroughly equip us for every good work that the Father has prepared for us to walk in.

The benchmark of guidance

God speaks to us primarily through His Word. The Word is the benchmark of Divine guidance against which all other 'voices' or 'revelations' must be measured. The written Word is the litmus test of all truth. Every leading, every prophecy, every vision and every doctrine must be submitted to and judged by The Word.

The Spirit of God authored the written Word. Therefore, whenever He speaks, it is always in unanimity with the Holy Scriptures.

'Your Word,' the Psalmist declared, *'is a lamp to my feet and a light to my path'* (Psalm 119:105). If we walk in the light of the Word we can be sure that we are walking in the will and purpose of God.

There are many voices in the world and none of them are without significance. If we are going to avoid the pitfalls of Satanic deception and walk in the true light of God, what manner of people ought we to be in spiritual wisdom and discernment?

I believe the answer is found in the Book of Acts, chapter seventeen, verses ten through twelve:

> *Then the brethren immediately sent Paul and Silas away by night to Berea. When they arrived, they went into the synagogue of the Jews. These were more fair-minded (mg: noble) than those in Thessalonica, in that they received the Word with all readiness, and SEARCHED THE SCRIPTURES DAILY TO FIND OUT WHETHER THOSE THINGS WERE SO. Therefore many of them believed, and also not a few of the Greeks, prominent women as well as men.*

Amen! May we be found meditating in God's Word day and night, observing to do according to all that is written in it. For then we will make our way prosperous and act wisely in the affairs of life!

12

The Witness Of The Spirit

'It is to your advantage that I go away,' Jesus told His disciples. To the uninitiated, such a statement would border on the incredible, if not the insane. How could life possibly be better WITHOUT Jesus? I am sure that this very question vexed the disciples' hearts and minds as they listened with bated breath to Jesus' words.

> *Nevertheless I tell you the truth. It is to your advantage that I go away; for if I do not go away, the Helper will not come to you; but if I depart, I will send Him to you...I still have many things to say to you, but you cannot bear them now. However, when He, the Spirit of truth, has come, He will guide you into all truth; for He will not speak on His own authority, but whatever He hears He will speak; and He will tell you things to come. He will glorify Me, for He will take of what is Mine and declare it to you.* (John 16:7,12–14)

The miracle of the New Birth and the Baptism of the Holy Spirit means that God is not only with us, but IN US! The Holy Spirit takes up residence in the redeemed, re-created spirit of every man and woman who submits to the Lordship of Jesus Christ. And the Spirit lives in us for one express purpose: to glorify Jesus in and through our lives!

It is the Spirit who transforms us into the image of the Lord Jesus Christ, from glory to glory (2 Corinthians 3:18).

It is the Spirit who empowers us for service (Acts 1:8). And it is the Spirit who guides us into all truth and tells us things to come.

'All truth' and 'things to come' refer to the plans and purposes of God for His Church as a whole and for each one of us individually, as members of His Body.

Spiritual perception

In the beginning God created man in His image and according to His likeness. Man was created as a spirit being, capable of partaking of God's life and nature, capable of thinking God's thoughts, speaking God's words and exercising God's power—capable of ruling over the earth on God's behalf. He lived in perfect fellowship with the Father and did only that which the Spirit prompted him to do, thus pleasing the Lord in every way.

However, when man violated God's command and sinned, the light of God went out in his spirit. He became 'spiritually dead'—alienated from the Presence and life of God. His mind was darkened—he became susceptible to the promptings and suggestions of the evil one. He lost contact with the realm of the Holy Spirit and could no longer hear the voice of God. The light of Divine revelation was extinguished. The Glory had departed and man was plunged into a terrible darkness.

Natural man depends almost entirely on his five senses for information and knowledge. Thus, the Bible describes him as 'carnal', which means, 'flesh-ruled'. The Bible further declares that it is impossible for a natural man, through the gateway of his physical senses, to know God or to receive the things of the Spirit of God:

> *Eye has not seen, nor ear heard, nor have entered into the heart of man the things which God has prepared for*

> *those who love Him.... But the natural man does not receive the things of the Spirit of God, for they are foolishness to him; nor can he know them, because they are spiritually discerned.* (1 Corinthians 2:9,14)

But thanks be to God, through the miracle of the New Birth God has again shone in our hearts to give the light of the knowledge of the glory of God in the face of Jesus Christ! (2 Corinthians 4:6). And furthermore, now we have *'this treasure in earthen vessels'*—the indwelling Spirit of God, who reveals the things that have been freely given to us by God.

The Spirit of God searches all things, yes, the deepest thoughts and intents of the Father's heart. He alone perfectly understands the Father's will and purpose for the lives of His children. And He has come to abide within us as 'The voice of God', to declare to us the things which He hears from the Father. Through the revelation of the indwelling Spirit we can have the mind of Christ! (1 Corinthians 2:10–16).

The umpire of peace

How does the Holy Spirit speak to us? The Bible declares that the things of the Spirit must be 'spiritually discerned'; in other words, they must be revealed to one's heart.

The eighth chapter of Romans gives us a detailed picture of 'Life in the Spirit'. Verse 8, in particular, gives us insight into how the Holy Spirit guides a believer into 'all truth':

> *The Spirit Himself bears witness with our spirit that we are children of God.*

The Spirit Himself bears witness WITH OUR SPIRIT! The Spirit of God does not bear witness with one's head, but with one's heart. The Holy Spirit dwells within the redeemed, re-created human spirit. And it is to the redeemed, re-created human spirit that the Holy Spirit reveals the knowledge of God.

The Spirit speaks to us in His own 'still, small voice' (1 Kings 19:12). Sometimes we are not still enough or small enough to hear! He will also speak to us through other supernatural means such as Prophecy, the Word of Knowledge, the Word of Wisdom, the Gift of Discernment, dreams, visions and revelations. However, as we have already noted, all of these things must be submitted to and judged by the unchanging Word of God.

One invariable sign of the Spirit's leading is what the Bible calls 'THE PEACE OF GOD'.

And let the peace of God rule in your hearts, to which you were also called in one body; and be thankful.
(Colossians 3:15)

The word 'rule' literally means, 'to arbitrate' or 'to act as umpire'. The voice of the Word and the Spirit should preside over all other voices in one's life. And the sure witness of the Spirit will ALWAYS produce a CERTAIN PEACE in one's heart. That 'peace' is more than a good feeling; it is the deep assurance and unwavering conviction that what one is contemplating is in fact, the will of God.

When this witness of the Spirit called 'peace' is absent, it is a sure sign that all is not well and that we should not proceed any further.

If we disregard the Spirit's restraint and persist in our own will and desire, we will invariably suffer the consequences. The Spirit not only understands God's plan for one's life, He also looks ahead with perfect foresight and sees the consequence of one's actions and decisions. He is totally committed to our wholeness in Christ Jesus, and to that end He warns, corrects, reproves and instructs us. Obeying the voice of the Spirit will not only bring glory to God, it may also save your life!

Notice that the Bible charges us with the responsibility of heeding the witness of the Spirit: *'LET the peace of God rule in your hearts....'* The Spirit is faithful to bear witness with our spirit, but we must give heed to His voice, submit to His Lordship and obey His Word. If we violate the peace of God, it will be to our own detriment.

Sensitivity of heart

'Spiritual sensitivity' or 'sensitivity of heart' is one of life's most precious possessions. Solomon prayed for it (1 Kings 3:9). Jesus was grieved that the religious people of His day lacked it (Mark 3:5). It must be sought after, cultivated and protected.

Spiritual sensitivity is commensurate with obedience. Every step of obedience is a step closer to Jesus and a step forward in the power of the Holy Spirit (John 14:21).

May God grant that we will become so sensitive to the gentle pressure of the 'Heavenly Dove' that like Jesus, we will be EASILY MOVED by the Spirit to do the Father's will.

13

The Providence Of God

The bottom line of all truth is that 'God is sovereign'. He regulates all things by the word of His power. He rules in the affairs of men and nations. He does according to His will in the army of heaven and among the inhabitants of the earth. No one can restrain His hand or say to Him, 'What have you done?' (Daniel 4:35).

Our faith must rest in the providence of God, as revealed in His Word. If we commit our lives into God's hands by giving first place to His Word, observing His commandments and walking in His counsel, and by obeying the voice of the Holy Spirit Who bears witness with our spirit concerning the will of God, we can then trust God to order our lives and circumstances in accordance with His purpose.

> *Trust in the Lord with all your heart, and lean not on your own understanding; in all your ways acknowledge Him, and He shall direct* (make straight) *your paths.*
> (Proverbs 3:5,6)

Please notice the conditions that precede God's providential guidance: complete trust in and dependence on God, and constant acknowledgement of and reverence for the Lord. God delights to show Himself strong on behalf of such a one whose heart is perfect toward Him!

Of this we can be certain: when it is God's will for something to happen, providing we are willing and obedient, HE will bring it to pass. It is not up to us to make things happen or to force doors open. We are called to wait on the Lord and to keep His way; HE will exalt us to inherit the land (Psalm 37:34).

The Lordship of Christ

'Jesus is Lord' is not a Christian slogan; it is an eternal fact. The Church must come to understand that Jesus Christ is Lord in all of life. He really does have 'all authority' in heaven AND ON EARTH! (Matthew 28:18).

As universal Lord, He holds all things in His hand. He is well able to order the steps and direct the ways of His people. He most certainly can ordain the circumstances of one's life, even down to the minutest details, in accordance with the will of the Father.

To the Church in Philadelphia Jesus declared:

> *These things says He who is holy, He who is true, 'He who has the key of David, He who opens and no one shuts, and shuts and no one opens': 'I know your works. See, I have set before you an open door, and no one can shut it; for you have a little strength, have kept My word, and have not denied My name'.* (Revelation 3:7,8)

It is important to remember that the Lord Jesus, in His God-appointed authority, not only 'opens', but also 'shuts' doors. We must be prepared for Him to open new doors and shut old ones; to open right doors and shut wrong ones!

The Apostle Paul demonstrated his faith in the providential guidance of God when he wrote to the Christians in Rome:

> *And we know that in all things God works for the good*

of those who love Him, who have been called according to His purpose. (Romans 8:28, NIV)

Our ultimate security is in knowing God and trusting His sovereignty over our lives!

Learning to 'tell the time'

Perhaps one of the most difficult aspects of the will of God for Christians to come to grips with is the Lord's timing. Even the prophets of old struggled with a sense of timing as they prophesied of the suffering of Christ and the glories that would follow (1 Peter 1:11).

God has a different appreciation of time than we human beings. He sits in heaven and looks from eternity into time. We live on earth and look from time into eternity, and sometimes we can't even see that far!

The Apostle Peter highlighted the great difference between the eternal and the temporal perspectives:

> *But, beloved, do not forget this one thing, that with the Lord one day is as a thousand years, and a thousand years as one day.* (2 Peter 3:8)

But Peter goes on to say, *'The Lord is not slack concerning His promise.'* God never loses track of time, nor is He ever late for an appointment. There is an appointed time for every purpose under heaven (Ecclesiastes 3:1). *'Though it tarries,'* the Lord says, *'WAIT FOR IT; because it will surely come, it will not delay unnecessarily'* (Habakkuk 2:3).

'You have need of patience' (Hebrews 10:36). How true! And in the meantime, how should we then live?

> *And let us not grow weary while doing good, for IN*

DUE SEASON we shall reap if we do not lose heart. (Galatians 6:9)

The times and season are in the Father's hand (Acts 1:7). In due season, at the appointed time, the Lord will bring to pass His will and fulfil His promise. As you wait on the Lord, do not grow weary or become discouraged, but keep your eyes fixed on Jesus, the Author and Perfecter of your faith. And keep offering the sacrifice of praise and thanksgiving because, *'Faithful is He who called you, who also will do it!'* (1 Thessalonians 5:24).

A word of advice

In conclusion, may I offer a simple, yet practical word of advice to all genuine seekers of God's will: Wait on the Lord for the three witnesses to 'take their stand'. Make sure you are acting on the clear instruction of God's Word. Make sure you have the witness of the Spirit and the peace of God in your heart. And make sure that the providential hand of God is evidently resting on your life, opening doors and preparing the way in which you should walk.

Sometimes one may find that although the witness of the Word and the witness of the Spirit are present, circumstances have not yet come into line. This is usually an indication that the timing is not quite right. Be patient and wait on the Lord. Don't give up and don't act presumptuously. Keep your eyes on Jesus for, *'He who believes on Him will by no means be put to shame!'*

14

Birthing The Will Of God Through Intercessory Prayer

Throughout the Bible, prayer is bound together with the fulfilment of God's will. Under the Old Covenant, God revealed His secrets to His servants the prophets. The prophets were not only called upon to proclaim the Word of the Lord, they were also responsible to intercede for its fulfilment!

Men like Daniel, Jeremiah, Isaiah and Hosea had supernatural revelation of God's plans and purposes. That revelation brought them to their knees and drove them to intercessory prayer. As a result they were numbered, not only among Israel's greatest prophets, but also among her greatest intercessors! In the economy of God, prophetic revelation and intercessory prayer go hand in hand.

The knowledge of God's will is designed to move us to prayer. Whenever the Word of the Lord comes to us, whether it be in the form of Scripture, prophecy or vision, we need to respond with a passionate, *'Let it be to me according to Your Word!'* (Luke 1:38).

There is something about laying hold of God in prayer for the fulfilment of His will that is foundational to any move of God or work of His Spirit. Jesus highlighted this truth when He taught us to pray:

> *Our Father in heaven, Hallowed be Your name. Your Kingdom come. Your will be done on earth as it is in heaven.* (Matthew 6:9,10)

The Kingdom of God comes through prayer! The will of God is done as we pray!

Birth pains

> *Epaphras, who is one of you, a servant of Christ, greets you, always labouring fervently for you in prayers, that you may stand perfect and complete in all the will of God.* (Colossians 4:12)

The phrase 'laboring fervently' denotes spiritual conflict with adversaries antagonistic to the purposes of God. The Greek word *'agonizomai'* means 'to contend in gymnastic games', or 'to wrestle'.

The will of God must be 'birthed' through intercessory prayer. At times there may be a struggle against unseen forces of darkness which seek to hinder the purposes of God. To this end, we are told to *'put on the whole armour of God'* and to *'pray always with all kinds of prayer and supplication in the power of the Spirit'* (Ephesians 6:10–18). If we persist, we will prevail! Hallelujah!

The goal of Epaphras' intercession was that the Church in Colossae would *'stand firm, with a matured faith and with a sure conviction of all that is in accordance with God's will'*. (TCNT)

Thank God, IT IS POSSIBLE to be steadfast, IT IS POSSIBLE to attain spiritual maturity, and IT IS POSSIBLE to be fully assured of all that is God's will, through intercessory prayer!

Our confidence

> *Now this is the confidence that we have in Him, that if we ask anything according to His will, He hears us. And if*

we know that He hears us, whatever we ask, we know that we have the petitions that we have asked of Him.
(1 John 5:14,15)

We are to pray ACCORDING TO HIS WILL, and SO THAT HIS WILL MAY BE DONE on earth as it is in Heaven!

Such is the purpose and such is the power of Holy Spirit-anointed, Christ-centred, Bible-believing prayer. It will enable us to stand perfect and complete IN ALL THE WILL OF GOD! Amen.